Northrop F-5E & F-5F Tiger II
Alexandre Guedes
Introduction

In the 1950s Northrop designed a lightweight fighter/attack aircraft, the N-156, in combat single-seat (F) and two-seat training (T) versions, powered by two GE J85 engines. Fuselage design was according to the Area Rule. In 1961 a trainer version designated the T-38 Talon entered service, being one of only a few supersonic trainers. The N-156F prototype first flew in 1959 and entered production in 1963 as the F-5A "Freedom Fighter".

The F-5E Tiger II was an improved version, with extended wingspan and upgraded avionics giving better air-to air combat capabilities. Also a new version of the engines, the GE J85-21/21A, were used. The aircraft first flew in 1972. The F-5E won the International Fighter Aircraft contest (IFA) for a low-cost fighter for countries threatened by a conflict with opponents operating late versions of the MiG-21.

The F-5E was also built as a two-seat version, designated "F-5F", with the addition of the second (instructor's) cockpit. One of the M39A2 internal cannons was deleted and the nose was lengthened.

It was exported to many countries, e.g. Iran and South Vietnam, where they took part in the Vietnam war. Some were captured by the North Vietnamese army after the armistice in 1975.

The F-5E was also assembled under license in Taiwan and South Korea. Tiger IIs remain in widespread service with Bahrain, Brazil, Chile, Honduras, Indonesia, Iran, Jordan, Kenya, Malaysia, Mexico, Saudi Arabia, Singapore, Switzerland, Taiwan, Thailand, Tunisia, US Marine Corps and US Navy and Yemen. Reconnaissance F-5E variants are operated by Malaysia (RF-5E Tigereye), Singapore (RF-5S) and Taiwan (RF-5E Tigergazer).

Numerous update programmes are available to keep this important warplane viable until well into the 21st century. These upgrades offer a mix of new avionics and structural refurbishment of the airframe. Chile operates F-5Es upgraded with Israeli assistance to Tiger III standard; their advanced avionics – including Elta 2032 radar and hands on stick and throttle controls – give a level of combat capability matching that of the F-16. The FIAR Grifo F/X Plus multimode radar has been fitted to Singaporean F-5S aircraft and has also been selected for Brazil's F-5Es.

The F-5E served with the USAF from 1975 to 1990 as part of the 26th, 64th, 65th and 627th aggressor squadrons in the US and worldwide (UK-527th and Philippines-26th).

The F-5E was also notably used by the United States Navy as an aggressor training aircraft for its "Top Gun" pilot school at Miramar, California. The USMC purchased some ex-USAF F-5 models in 1989 to replace their F-2 l (Israeli Kfir) aggressors.

In all, 792 F-5E models were produced by Northrop factories. Northrop also added manufacture of 140 F-5F two-seat combat trainers and a further 12 RF-5E Tigereyes. Taiwan produced the F-5E/F-5F in quantity, some 308 aircraft deliveries in all. Switzerland also undertook local-license production of these new versions and produced 91 F-5E and F-5F models. South Korea added 68 local examples.

The F-5 was one of most successful export products of the US aviation industry.

F-5E preserved at Muzeum Lotnictwa Polskiego in Cracow, Poland. (Jarosław Dobrzyński)

Northrop F-5E Tiger II
USAF, s/n11419 of 58th TFTW, Luke AFB AZ, ca. 1979.

Aircraft aluminium overall. Yellow bands with black trim.

Northrop F-5E Tiger II
USAF, s/n11419 of 58th TFTW, Luke AFB AZ, ca. 1979.

Northrop F-5E Tiger II

Fuerza Aérea Mexicana (FAM), Mexican Air Force, 4506, *Esquadrón Aéreo 401*, Santa Lucia AB, 2014.

Camouflage pattern: Forest Green FS34102, Tan FS30219, Dark Green FS34079.

Northrop F-5E Tiger II

Fuerza Aérea Mexicana (FAM), Mexican Air Force, 4506, *Esquadrón Aéreo 401*, Santa Lucia AB, 2014.

Northrop F-5E Tiger II
Schweizer Luftwaffe, Suisse Air Force, *Fliegerstaffel* 19. 75th anniversary – September 2014.
Camouflage pattern: Flat Dark Gull Grey, Flat Gull Grey.

Northrop F-5E Tiger II
Schweizer Luftwaffe, Suisse Air Force, *Fliegerstaffel* 19. 75th anniversary – September 2014.

Northrop F-5E Tiger II
القوات الجوية اليمنية (*al-Quwwat al-Jawwiya al-Yamaniya*), Yemeni Air Force, 50608, Sana'a Air Base, 2010.

Camouflage pattern: Sand Yellow and Brown uppersurfaces with Grey undersurfaces.

Northrop F-5E Tiger II
Yemeni Air Force, 50608, Sana'a Air Base, 2010.

Northrop F-5E Tiger III
Fuerza Aérea de Chile, Chilean Air Force, 802, IV *Brigada Aérea, Grupo de Aviacion Nº* 12, 2012.
Camouflage pattern: Flat Dark Gull Grey, Flat Gull Grey.

Northrop F-5E Tiger III
Fuerza Aérea de Chile, 802, IV Brigada Aérea, Grupo de Aviacion Nº 12, 2012.

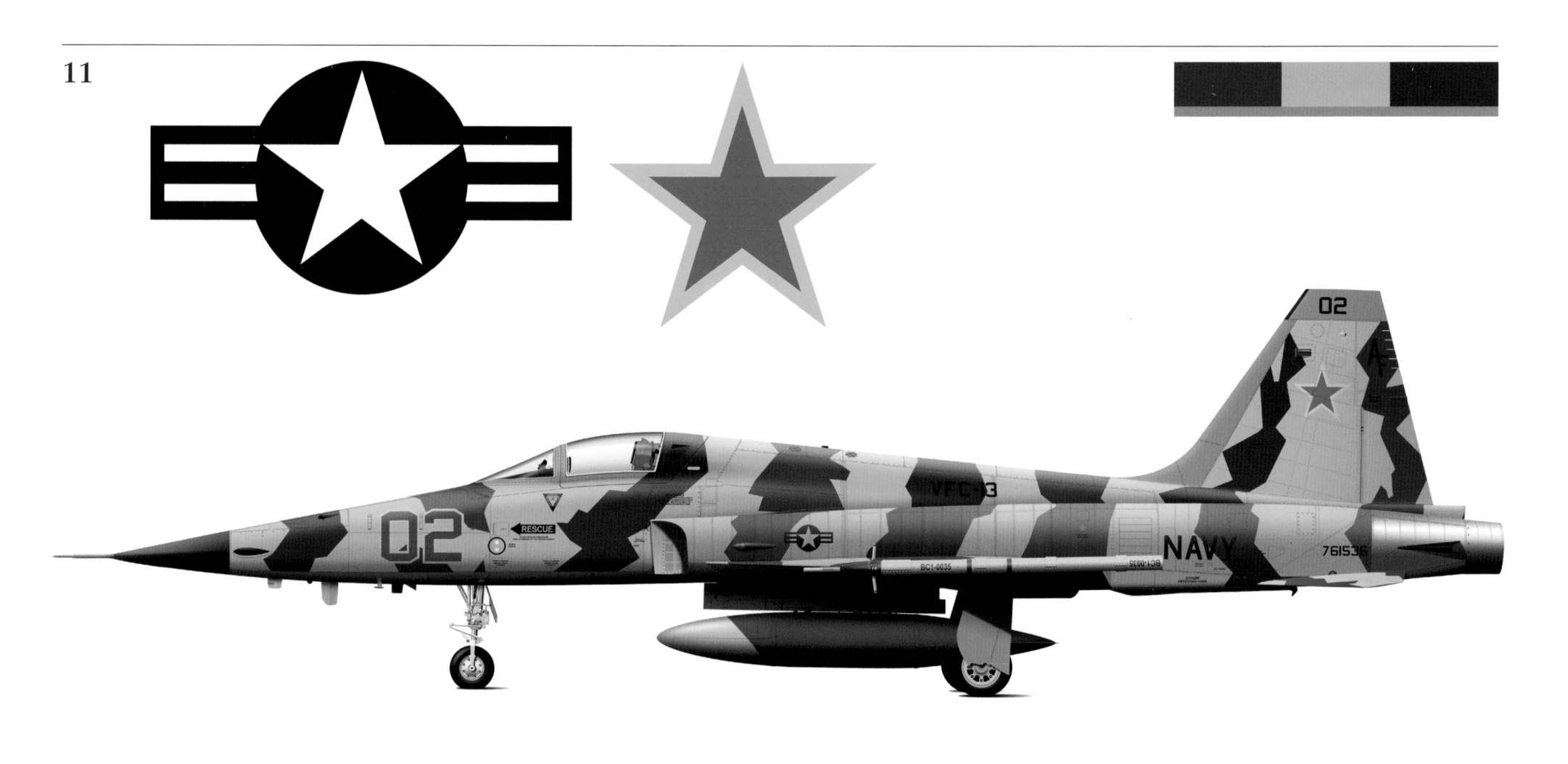

Northrop F-5N Tiger II
US NAVY, AF 02 – 761536, VFC-13, NAS Fallon, 2015.
Camouflage pattern: Field Drab (FS 30118), Sand (FS 33531), Green (FS 34258).

Northrop F-5N Tiger II
US NAVY, AF 02 – 761536, VFC-13, NAS Fallon, 2015.

Northrop F-5EM Tiger II
Força Aérea Brasileira (FAB), Brasilian Air Force, 4867, ALA 12, 1º GAVCA, Santa Cruz Air Base, 2016.
Camouflage pattern: Green (FS 34092) and Grey (FS 36176)

Northrop F-5EM Tiger II
Brasilian Air Force, 4867, ALA 12, 1º GAVCA, Santa Cruz Air Base, 2016.

Northrop F-5S Tiger II
Royal Singapore Air Force, RSAF, 819 – 144th Squadron, Paya Lebar Air Base, 2015.
Camouflage pattern: Flat Dark Gull Grey, Flat Gull Grey.

Northrop F-5S Tiger II
Royal Singapore Air Force, 819 – 144th Squadron, Paya Lebar Air Base, 2015.

Northrop F-5T Tiger III

قوات الجوية الملكية (*Al-quwwa al-jawwiya al-malikiyya al-maghribiyya*), Royal Moroccan Air Force, 91933, 2014.

Camouflage pattern: Dark Green (FS 34079), Sand Yellow (FS 20400), Brown (FS 30140) uppersurafces. Grey (FS 36622) undersurfaces.

Northrop F-5T Tiger III
Royal Moroccan Air Force, 91933, 2014.

Northrop RF-5E Tigereye II
Tentera Udara Diraja Malaysia, Malaysian Air Force, TDUM M29-19, 2012.
Camouflage pattern: Light Gray (FS 36373), Light Gray (FS 36495), Light Gull Gray (FS 36440).

Northrop RF-5E Tigereye II
Malaysian Air Force, TDUM M29-19, 2012.

Northrop F-5F Tiger II
US NAVY, AF 20 – 761580, VFC-13, NAS Fallon, 2014.

Aircraft Flat Black overall.

Northrop F-5F Tiger II
US NAVY, AF 20 – 761580, VFC-13, NAS Fallon, 2014.

Northrop F-5F Tiger II
Fuerza Aérea Hondureña (FAH), Honduran Air Force, 4002, 2014.

Camouflage pattern: Flat Dark Gull Grey, Flat Gull Grey uppersurfaces, Light Grey undersurfaces.

Northrop F-5F Tiger II
Honduran Air Force, 4002, 2014.

Northrop F-5F Tiger II
Tentara Nasional Indonesia-Angkatan Udara, TNI-AU, Indonesian Air Force, TL-0515, 2015.

Camouflage pattern: Light Blue, Blue-grey, Grey.

TL-0515

TNI AU

15

Northrop F-5F Tiger II
Indonesian Air Force, TL-0515, 2015.

Northrop F-5F Tiger II
Kenyan Air Force, 928, 2013.
Camouflage pattern: Green (FS 34092) and Grey (FS 36176).

Northrop F-5F Tiger II
Kenyan Air Force, 928, 2013.

Northrop F-5F Tiger II
ROCAF – Taiwan Air Force, 5374, 2014.

Camouflage pattern: Sierra Tan (FS 30219), Dark Green (FS 34079), Medium Green (FS 34102).

Northrop F-5F Tiger II
ROCAF – Taiwan Air Force, 5374, 2014.

Northrop F-5F Tiger II

القوات الجوية الملكية السعودية (*al-quwat al-jawwiyyah al-malakiyyah as-sudiyyah*), Royal Saudi Air Force, 326, 1991.

Camouflage pattern: Dark Earth (FS 30140), Tan (FS 20400) and Dark Green (FS 34079) uppersurfaces with Light Grey (36622) undersurfaces.

القوات الجوية الملكية السعودية
ROYAL SAUDI AIR FORCE

Northrop F-5F Tiger II
Royal Saudi Air Force, 326, 1991.

Northrop F-5F Tiger II
El Quwat ej-Jawiya et'Tunsia, Tunisian Air Force, Y 92502, 2012.

Camouflage pattern: Tan (FS 20400), Light Grey (36622) and Dark Green (FS 34079) uppersurfaces with Light Grey (36622) undersurfaces.

Northrop F-5F Tiger II
Tunisian Air Force, Y 92502, 2012.

Northrop F-5FM Tiger II

Força Aérea Brasileira (FAB), Brasilian Air Force, 4808, ALA 3, 1º/14º GAV, Canoas Air Base, 2016.

Camouflage pattern: Green (FS 34092) and Grey (FS 36176)

Northrop F-5FM Tiger II
Brasilian Air Force, 4808, ALA 3, 1º/14º GAV, Canoas Air Base, 2016.

Northrop F-5T Tiger II
Royal Singapore Air Force, RSAF, 853 – 144th Squadron, Paya Lebar Air Base, 2016.
Camouflage pattern: Flat Dark Gull Grey, Flat Gull Grey uppersurfaces, Light Grey undersurfaces.

Northrop F-5T Tiger II
Royal Singapore Air Force, 853 – 144th Squadron, Paya Lebar Air Base, 2016.

HESA آذرخش (Azarakhsh)

نیروی هوایی ارتش جمهوری اسلامی ایران, Islamic Republic of Iran Air Force, 3-7361, Vahtati AB, 2009.

Aircraft Olive Green (FS 34574) overall.

HESA Azarakhsh
Islamic Republic of Iran Air Force, 3-7361, Vahtati AB, 2009.

Northrop F-5E Tiger II
Kong Thap Akat Thai Royal, Thai Air Force,
RTAF, 90408 VM, 904th Squadron, Aggressor 08, Don Muang AFB, 1998.
Camouflage pattern: Light Blue International (FS 35109), Navy Blue 212 (FS 35164), Pale Green (FS 35414).

Northrop F-5E Tiger II
RTAF, 90408 VM, 904th Squadron, Aggressor 08, Don Muang AFB, 1998.

Published in Poland in 2017
by STRATUS sp.j.
Po. Box 123,
27-600 Sandomierz 1, Poland
e-mail: office@wydawnictwostratus.pl
as
MMPBooks,
3 Gloucester Close,
Petersfield,
Hampshire GU32 3AX
e-mail: office@mmpbooks.biz

© 2017 MMPBooks
http://www.mmpbooks.biz

ISBN 978-83-65281-59-3

Editor in chief
Roger Wallsgrove

Editorial Team
Bartłomiej Belcarz
Robert Pęczkowski
Artur Juszczak

Colour profiles
Alexandre Guedes

DTP
Artur Juszczak

Printed by
Drukarnia Diecezjalna,
ul. Żeromskiego 4,
27-600 Sandomierz
www.wds.pl
marketing@wds.pl

PRINTED IN POLAND

Also in this series.

SPOTLIGHT ON
P-51D MUSTANG
AMERICAN ACES
ARTUR JUSZCZAK

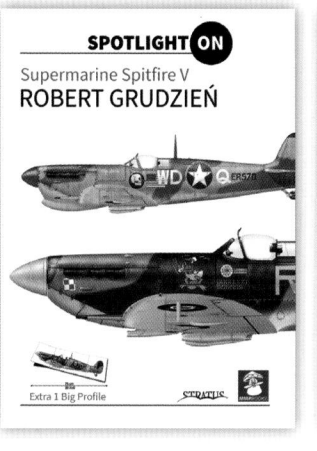

SPOTLIGHT ON
Supermarine Spitfire V
ROBERT GRUDZIEŃ

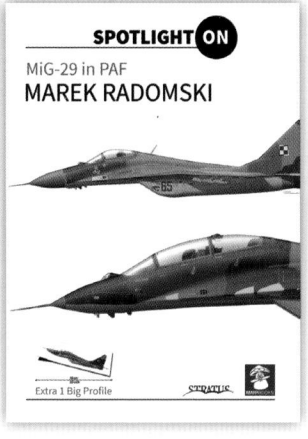

SPOTLIGHT ON
MiG-29 in PAF
MAREK RADOMSKI

SPOTLIGHT ON
Messerschmitt Bf 109 in Romania
TEODOR LIVIU MOROŞANU
DAN MELINTE

SPOTLIGHT ON
Junkers Ju 87 Stuka
SIMON SCHATZ

SPOTLIGHT ON
F4U Corsair
ZBIGNIEW KOLACHA

SPOTLIGHT ON
McDonnell Douglas
F-4E/EJ/F/G/RF-4E Phantom II
Striking colour schemes
JP VIEIRA

SPOTLIGHT ON
Yakovlev Yak-3
ARTUR JUSZCZAK